RELAXING AND RELATABLE: A FUNNY ADULT COLORING BOOK FOR EVERYDAY STRESS RELIEF

UNWIND WITH EVERYDAY LAUGHS AND EASY-TO-COLOR DESIGNS

EVE EVERGREEN

WELCOME & WHY THIS BOOK EXISTS

Have you ever opened your fridge, stared at a shelf of mystery leftovers, and thought, "Is this dinner, or am I auditioning for a survival show?" Or maybe you've had that moment of standing in front of the printer, begging it to cooperate, as if sheer willpower could overcome its treacherous nature. If you've nodded along or chuckled knowingly, you've come to the right place. Welcome to the delightful chaos of adulting.

This coloring book was created for everyone who's ever felt like they're juggling flaming swords while blindfolded. Life as an adult is full of everyday absurd moments.., from wondering why there's always one sock missing to realizing you have Googled "how to boil an egg" for the third time this year. It's messy, hilarious, and many times overwhelming. But - that's part of the fun.

When life feels like it's spinning out of control—or just spinning in circles—it helps to take a step back, laugh at the madness, and find a moment of calm. That's where this book comes in. It's a place to pause, breathe, and embrace the wonderfully ridiculous parts of life.

Coloring isn't just for kids - studies show that adult coloring can reduce stress, promote mindfulness, and give us a break from the never-ending to-do list. But this isn't about science—it's about joy. It's about letting go of perfection, laughing at how many tabs your brain has open, and celebrating the small wins, like remembering to water your plants... or at least most of them.

So grab a pen, pencil, or crayon—whatever speaks to you. Dive into these pages, bring them to life, and remember: even when adulting is hard, you're doing better than you think. And hey, if all else fails, you've got a questionable casserole waiting in the fridge.

THE STRUGGLE IS REAL: EMBRACING RELATABLE CHAOS

Let's be honest—adulting is not the glamorous adventure we thought it would be when we were kids. Back then, we dreamed of staying up late, eating whatever we wanted, and calling the shots. Now? Staying up late means feeling like a zombie the next day, eating "whatever we want" often involves expired yogurt or cereal for dinner, and calling the shots? That's just another way of saying we have bills to pay.

Life as an adult is a never-ending cycle of juggling responsibilities, forgetting half of them, and wondering why you're so tired all the time. It's a battle between trying to stay on top of everything while also Googling "how long can I leave wet laundry in the washer?" for the tenth time. But amidst the chaos, there's something beautiful—humor. Because if we don't laugh at the absurdity of it all, we might cry (or scream at our Wi-Fi router).

Take, for instance, the phenomenon of having "too many tabs open" in your brain. One moment, you're trying to focus on work, and the next, you're mentally jumping between questions like, "Did I reply to that email?" "What's for dinner?" and "Do I need to Google if this mold is dangerous?" It's a mental traffic jam, and we've all been there. The good news? You're not alone in your mental multitasking marathon—every adult is sprinting in the same race.

And what about the fridge? Ah, the fridge. It's both a treasure chest and a graveyard. You open it, hoping for inspiration, only to find questionable casseroles, half-eaten desserts, and a single shriveled carrot in the corner. You think, "Why did I buy so much food?" while simultaneously deciding there's absolutely nothing to eat. It's a comedy sketch that plays out in kitchens everywhere.

Also, there's the "never-ending checklist of responsibilities." Some days, you're just proud you got out of bed, brushed your teeth, and managed not to yell at your printer. (Seriously, why are printers so evil?)

These small wins may seem insignificant, but in reality, they are the proof that you're conquering the little hurdles of daily life. Celebrating these moments, no matter how small, is essential to surviving—and thriving—in adulthood.

The truth is, nobody has this all figured out. Instagram might make it look like everyone else is acing life with perfect homes, well-behaved pets, and color-coded calendars, but don't be fooled. Behind the scenes, everyone has their version of an "empty fridge syndrome" moment or a "why is this happening to me?" day.

This is exactly where this coloring book comes in.

It's a reminder that life does not have to be perfect all the time to be beautiful (or hilarious). These pages celebrate all the moments that make us shake our heads, laugh, or just sigh and say, "Yep, that's life." So go ahead, pick a page, and let the chaos of everyday life inspire your creativity. And remember, the struggle is real—but so is the joy in laughing at it.

WHY HUMOR AND COLORING WORK TOGETHER

Have you ever noticed how a good laugh can make even the worst day a little better? Humor has this magical way of taking the edge off life's challenges.., turning the "Oh no!" moments into "Oh well!" moments. If a little creativity are added into into the mix, you've got the perfect recipe for stress relief. That's exactly why this coloring book exists: to combine all the calming benefits of coloring with the joy of laughing at life's quirks.

There's actual science behind this, believe it or not. Laughter releases a feel good chemical like endorphin, which instantly boosts your mood. At the same time, creative activities like coloring engage your brain in a way that helps you focus and relax. It's the ultimate mind trick —while you're choosing colors for that brain full of tabs or that fridge full of leftovers, your stress levels are quietly dropping, and your mind is finding its happy place.

But what makes this combination of humor and coloring truly special is how it lets you embrace imperfection. Adulting is messy, and let's be real: so is coloring. You're bound to color outside the lines sometimes, and that's okay—just like it's okay if you didn't fold the laundry for three days or accidentally put the milk in the pantry. Life is about doing your best, laughing at the rest, and finding joy in the little things.

Think of these coloring pages as your permission slip to let go. Feel free to add your own twist—color the brain tabs in neon, scribble in a new label on the fridge, or turn the adulting checklist into your personal manifesto. This is your chance to take everyday chaos and make it beautiful (or at least brightly colored).

The best part? There's no "right" way to do this. Whether you're using pencils, markers, or even crayons you borrowed from your kid's stash, the goal isn't perfection—it's connection. Connection to your creative side, to the humor in your life, and to the realization that everyone else is stumbling through adulthood just like you are.

So grab your favorite coloring tools, pick a page that speaks to you, and let the laughter and creativity flow. Because when life hands you chaos, sometimes the best response is to color it in.

TIPS FOR ENJOYING THE COLORING BOOK

Ready to dive in and start coloring? Great! Before you begin, here are some tips to help you make the most of this experience.

1. Please Give Yourself Permission not to be perfect

First things first: there's no such thing as "messing up" when it comes to coloring. The wrong color? That's just a creative flair.

Or did you accidentally colored outside the lines? Congratulations—you have embraced spontaneity! Just like life is, this book is not about getting everything perfect. It's about showing up, doing your best, and having fun along the way…

2. Make It a Self-Care Moment

Your coloring time should be turned into acts of self-love. Pour yourself a cup of coffee, tea, or maybe even a glass of wine (we won't judge). Settle into your favorite chair, wrap yourself in a cozy blanket, and take a deep breath. This is *your* time, free from emails, to-do lists, and the 18 other tabs your brain is trying to manage.

3. Set the Mood

Want to make your coloring session even better? Set the stage! Put on your favorite playlist—whether that's soothing instrumental music, a nostalgic throwback to the '90s, or a stand-up comedy special that makes you laugh until your sides hurt. Light a candle, dim the lights, or leave the TV on in the background if that helps you relax. Whatever feels good, go with it.

4. Color Outside the Lines—Literally and Figuratively

While the book gives you a starting point, it's yours to personalize. Add your own touch to the pages. Maybe your brain tabs need a "Did I leave the stove on?" label. Or perhaps your fridge needs an extra shelf of "Emergency Chocolate" or "Random Sauce Collection." This is your chance to make the book as funny, relatable, and uniquely *you* as possible.

5. Make It Social (or Not)

Coloring doesn't have to be a solo activity. Invite friends over for a coloring night, share your completed pages on social media, or use it as a way to bond with your kids (who will probably try to "help" by taking over a page). On the other hand, if you prefer your "me time," keep this as your little retreat from the world. It's all about what works for you.

6. Celebrate the Small Wins

Every page you complete is a win. Think of it as a metaphor for adulting: some days, you get through an entire page without a hitch; other days, you only color one small section, but you still showed up. Whether you finish one page or ten, you're creating something beautiful —and giving yourself a well-deserved break in the process.

7. Don't Rush

Life is fast-paced enough as it is. This book is your permission to slow down. Remember to ake your time with each page. Choose colors thoughtfully or grab whatever pen is closest—it's up to you. There's no deadline, no pressure, and absolutely no need to finish in one sitting.

Are you ready to grab your markers, your pencils, or crayons and dive in? Remember, this isn't just a coloring book—it's a celebration of life's little quirks, a way to unwind, and a reminder that you're doing great, even when it doesn't feel like it. Now go forth, laugh a little, color a lot, and enjoy the ride. You've earned it!

CONNECTION AND COMMUNITY

One of the best things about the chaos of adulting is that you're not alone in it. Every time you've groaned at an empty fridge, forgotten what you walked into a room for, or silently cursed your Wi-Fi for betraying you, someone else has been right there, experiencing the same thing. That shared struggle is what makes adulthood both maddening and deeply hilarious.

This coloring book is more than just a collection of pages—it's a way to connect with those universal experiences. It's a reminder that no matter how messy life gets, we're all in it together. Everyone has their version of "too many tabs open," and everyone has stared at a "questionable casserole" in their fridge at least once. The beauty is in finding the humor and realizing you're part of a larger community of people who get it.

Want to take it one step further? Share your creativity with others! Snap a picture of your finished pages (or even your works in progress) and send them to friends or post them on social media. Create a virtual laugh fest by adding your own captions or twists to the designs. Better yet, start a hashtag like #RelatableColoringClub or #AdultingInColor and see how others are bringing these pages to life.

If you're feeling particularly bold, make it a group activity! Invite friends over for a "Color and Wine" night, where you can swap stories about printer struggles, laundry catastrophes, and your latest adulting victories (like actually folding your clothes after washing them). Coloring can be a surprisingly social activity, and sharing the humor makes it even more fun.

And for those of you who prefer to keep things private, that's great too. Think of this book as your little oasis from the demands of the world: a safe space to laugh at yourself, to color outside the lines, and remember that even when life feels overwhelming, you're doing better than you think.

This book isn't just about coloring—it's about connection. This book will help you to connect to your creative side, to the humor in life's awkward moments, and to the comforting thought that none of us really have it all figured out. So whether you want to share your coloured masterpieces with the world or keep them just for yourself, know that you're part of a bigger story: the hilarious, colorful journey of adulting.

Next, take up your coloring pencils, and start filling those pages with color and laughter. Let's make the everyday struggles of life something worth celebrating.

LAST BUT NOT LEAST: A CLOSING PEP TALK

You are doing great.

Really.

Adulting is not about having all the answers (altough many people think so) - it is more about figuring things out on your on way. It's about showing up every day, even when you're running on caffeine and (questionable) leftovers. It's about all the small wins, finding a matching pair of socks, replying to that email, or to resist the urge to throw your printer out the window. These small wins are not insignificant, they all add up to something extraordinary:

YOU, navigating the chaos with resilience, humor, and a whole lot of heart.

This coloring book is your permission to take a break. Laugh at all the quirks of life, Let go of perfection, and also, color your way through the hilarity of everyday struggles. This book is your reminder that even when things feel overwhelming, there's always room for a little humor, creativity, and self-care.

So the next time your brain feels like it has too many tabs open, or your fridge looks like the land of forgotten leftovers, remember this: you're not alone. We're all stumbling through adulthood together, one mismatched sock and one small victory at a time. And if we can laugh along the way—even better.

Now, go forth and color your world, both inside and out... Whether you choose bright, bold colors or calming pastel tones, make it yours. Life is not always picture-perfect, but it's still a masterpiece in progress! *And trust me, you're absolutely nailing it. Let's get coloring!*

I'm not procrastinating; I'm prioritizing tomorrow's problems

Label your own brain tabs!

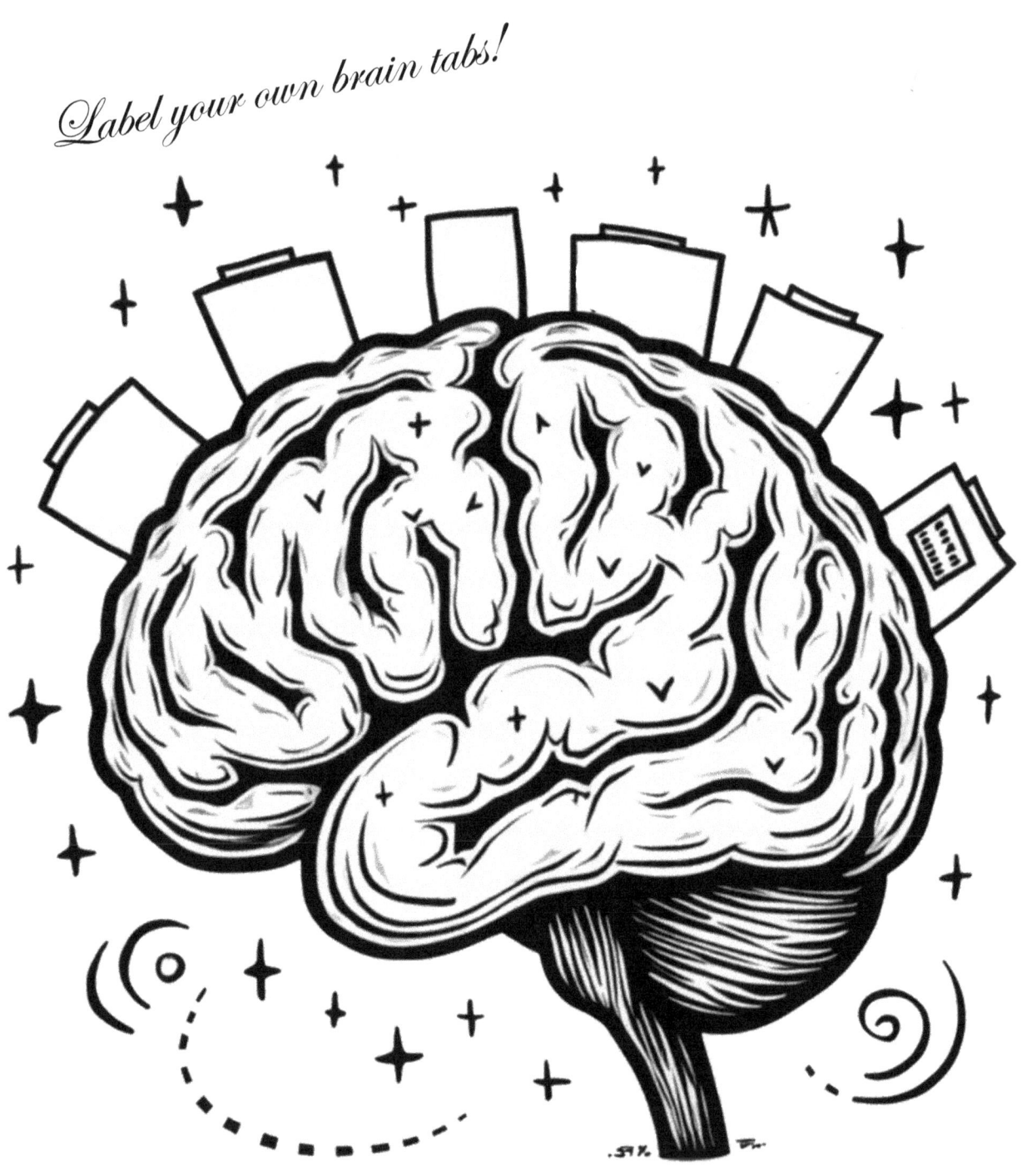

Too many tabs open, not enough RAM!

Build Your Own Excuse Generator

Daily Wins
- Didn't yell at the printer
- Remembered passwords (well, one of them)
- Watered the plant (okay, some of them)

Studies show; 9 out of 10 printers are plotting against us.

Emergency Fridge Inventory
- Expired yogurt (x3)
- Mysterious sauce (unlabelled)
- Leftover pizza (probably fine)
- That one sad vegetable

This casserole isn't questionable—it's a test of courage.

80% of adults agree: Fridge the where leftovers to to die.

Laundry Baskets proof that chores are never really done

Laundry today, or naked tomorrow—life is full of tough decisions!

A tornado of tasks with space to doodle your own responsibilities.

Adulthood is basically Googling how to do stuff while trying not to cry

Checklist: Am I an Adult Yet?
- Paid a bill ✅
- Folded laundry (or thought about it) ✅
- Resisted throwing phone across room ✅
- Googled "how to be an adult" ✅

If adulting came with a manual, I'd still lose it

Funny_Word_Search_Puzzle

	0	1	2	3	4	5	6	7	8	9	10	11	12	13	14
B	W	O	R	Z	P	O	M	K	S	S	O	M	M	G
I	J	J	G	B	P	F	N	A	I	L	G	U	G	L
L	R	Z	E	R	Z	U	W	B	F	V	G	B	F	V
V	Q	V	O	J	K	D	F	V	V	S	N	N	Z	X
S	T	D	Y	F	I	J	R	S	C	H	R	K	D	Y
Q	U	C	U	R	W	G	W	V	H	J	C	I	X	P
X	L	H	K	A	V	J	V	K	S	L	L	X	Z	L
K	Q	A	V	P	S	B	H	Q	M	P	X	V	D	E
H	H	O	L	U	R	F	K	B	O	C	C	Y	I	O
G	P	X	U	L	R	I	T	O	P	S	F	U	U	V
R	L	T	Q	V	A	T	V	V	Z	I	L	E	A	O
F	Y	Z	Q	U	T	A	L	R	J	M	A	U	J	Z
V	B	I	X	O	I	L	Z	A	W	P	I	H	G	Z
H	T	Y	Y	F	D	Y	S	W	T	M	Z	H	M	Z
M	K	T	B	Q	P	A	S	T	G	W	Y	W	T	P

Here are the words you can search for in the puzzle:
Procrastinate, Printer, Laundry, Yogurt, Chaos, Meetings, Password, Wifi, Taxes, Caffeine, Reboot, Budget, Email, Snacks, Vacuum
You can look for these words in all directions: horizontally, vertically, diagonally, and even backward! Enjoy the hunt!